DENMARK
is my country

Bernice and Cliff Moon

My Country

America is my country
Australia is my country
Britain is my country
China is my country
Denmark is my country
France is my country
India is my country
Israel is my country
Italy is my country
New Zealand is my country
Spain is my country

Further titles are in preparation

*This book is based on an original text
and photographs by Ulla Andersen.
The cover picture was supplied by ZEFA.*

First published in 1984 by
Wayland (Publishers) Ltd
49 Lansdowne Place, Hove
East Sussex BN3 1HF, England

© Copyright 1984 Wayland (Publishers) Ltd

ISBN 0 85078 416 6

Phototypeset by Kalligraphics Ltd, Redhill, Surrey
Printed in Italy by G. Canale & C.S.p.A., Turin
Bound in the UK by The Pitman Press, Bath

Contents

I'm Birger and I'm a journalist.

Forty-eight newspapers are published in Denmark every day.
I live in Frederikssund on the island of Zealand and
I work for a morning newspaper which is full of news
about Frederikssund and the places nearby.
You probably have a local paper in the place where you live.

This is the office where
I write all the reports
for my newspaper.

Every year the people of Frederikssund put on
a play about Vikings.
Here is my family all dressed up for last year's play.

Most people know what is going on in the world from radio or TV.
At the moment we only have one television channel in Denmark.
However, there are plans to start some local TV stations and
these will show the same kind of news as our newspaper.
I am very interested in local television and
I hope I can help to make it work well.

I am Kasper and I'm looking for a job.

I live at Rødding in the part of Denmark called Jutland.
I trained to be a printer but I can't get a job so
I'm using my time to study at a high school.
We have 90 folk high schools in Denmark and
all kinds of people go to them to study.

This is the Rødding
Folk High School where
I am a student.

But what is a folk high school?
Danish people are very keen to learn more about their country
and all kinds of other things they didn't learn at school.
So women and men of any age can go to a folk high school.
I am studying religion, pottery, farming and Danish.
I'm glad there are no exams at the end of my courses
because I can learn things just for fun.

These are the students in my pottery class.
Everyone has a potter's wheel and plenty of space to work in.

My name is Marie and I'm a pensioner.

I am 88 years old and I live with my husband, Hilmar,
at Jullerup on the island of Funen.
We have been married for 65 years and
we got a letter from Queen Margrethe II of Denmark
on our wedding anniversary.

Our grandchildren often
come to see us.
I love playing cards so
we always have a game
when they come.

This is our little red-brick house and that's Hilmar
standing on the path looking at our garden.

My husband was the village postman before he retired.
I thought things might be difficult when he stopped work
but the Danish government looks after old people.
We both get pensions which come from the taxes we paid
throughout our working lives.
If we had no savings we would get help with the rent and
we could have a free telephone and someone to clean the house.
We are glad that we can live in our own home and
we love to see our children, grandchildren and
great-grandchildren when they come to visit us.

11

My name is Knud and I'm a pig farmer.

I wonder whether you've eaten any Danish bacon this week?
We think that Danish bacon is the best and
I should know because I have 1,000 pigs on my farm.

I seem to spend most of my time feeding hungry pigs.

The pigs on my farm are not very fat but
we get large hams from them when they are killed.
Danish pigs have two more ribs than other breeds of pig and
this makes their bodies longer.
Their meat is used either for bacon, tinned ham,
pork sausages or pork joints.
I feed the pigs on barley which I grow myself.
But my pigs eat more barley than I can grow so
I have to buy extra for them.
We also rear a lot of piglets on the farm.
I have about 70 one-year-old sows and
they give birth to about 1,200 piglets a year.

This is my farm in the
west of Zealand island.
In winter the snow
covers our fields and
it is very cold.

I am John and I'm an electronics worker.

Next time you see a shop which sells radios, TV or hi-fi,
look out for the name Bang and Olufsen.
That's the firm I work for at Struer in Jutland.
Three-quarters of our sets are sold to other countries.

My job is to test
the printed circuits of
television sets to see
that they work properly.

All our television sets are tested before they leave the factory.

I live at Holstebro and every morning I drive 15 km (9 miles)
to the Bang and Olufsen factory at Struer.
A third of the families in Struer have someone working
in the factory so the company means a lot to the town.
We also have branches in ten other countries.
Electronics is one of the industries that is growing
very quickly at the moment.

I'm Merete and I'm a student.

I am a student at Copenhagen University.
Copenhagen is the capital city of Denmark and
it is very large and very beautiful.
Many people call it the 'City of Spires' because
there are so many church spires and towers.
I have been studying history here for four years now.
One of the most exciting times in the history of Denmark
was when the Vikings lived here.
All over Denmark you will find Viking forts and
graves where the Vikings buried their dead.
Bronze Age people lived in Denmark before the Vikings.
They built large mounds where they buried their dead and
you can still see them in many parts of Denmark.

I have a part-time job
at this museum in Roskilde.
You can see five
Viking ships here.

There are 700 Viking graves
here at Lindholm and
they are 1,000 years old.

17

My name is John and I am a fisherman.

I am the skipper of a trawler which is based at Esbjerg.
Many fishing boats in Denmark are still made of wood but
mine is made of iron.
We drag a large net called a trawl behind us
when we go fishing on the Dogger Bank in the North Sea.

I have a crew of three
on my trawler.
Here you can see them
unloading a large catch
of North Sea cod.

Esbjerg is on the west coast of Jutland and
it is the biggest fishing port in Denmark.
We usually catch what fishermen call 'trash fish'.
Trash fish is used to make animal foods, oil and fish meal.
Most of our catch is sand eel and herring but
other fish find their way into our nets as well.
We sort them out and if there are any fish that can be eaten
we sell them at a higher price.

This is a trailer-load of trash fish.

My name is Kurt
I am a teacher.

I'm in charge of fifteen children at a day care centre.
It is in Copenhagen and we look after children
from the ages of two to twelve.

About 10,000 people live in this new housing area in Copenhagen.
Children from these flats come to our day care centre.

Many parents of our children work in the centre of Copenhagen
and often they don't get home until quite late.
They need someone to look after their children for a day.
Some of our children are here from 7.00 a.m. until 5.00 p.m.
That's a very long day when you're only two years old!
We make breakfast for the children who come very early.
At 9 o'clock we have an assembly and read the register.
I love taking the children out for trips.
We play games, sing and talk about everything we see.

I'm Elisabeth.
I'm a priest.

I became a priest six years ago and now
I am the Vicar of Farum in Copenhagen.
There are two churches in my parish — one old and one new.
The new church has lots of rooms where I have meetings
for younger and older children.
At the moment I'm starting a youth club.
I try to show people how to help others.
People in some countries think it is very strange
to have female priests.
But there are now many of us in Denmark and
we are quite well accepted.

Here you can see me
telling our scout troop
about the new youth club
I am starting in Farum.

This is the old church
in my parish.
It is more than
700 years old.

My name is Frede and I work in a brewery.

I have worked at the Faxe brewery in Fakse
for forty years and I'll be retiring soon.
I'm only 61 years old but I shall get a good pension and
it will give a younger person the chance of a job.

 All these empty bottles
will be filled with beer
here at the Faxe brewery.

Fakse is built on chalk and the underground water
is the best in the world for making beer and soft drinks.
We pump water to the factory from about a dozen wells.
We are only allowed to sell bottled beer in Denmark
because bottles can be used again and again.
Our canned beer is sold to other countries, including Britain.

This is a Faxe brewery lorry delivering beer.
We have a fleet of lorries like this one.

My name is Preben and I am a forestry worker.

I work in the Rold Forest which is in northern Jutland. It's the largest stretch of forest in Denmark and thousands of people come to visit it every year.

This is our nursery in the Rold Forest. We grow one million young trees here every year.

We have lots of tall, old beech trees in the forest.
There are a few oak and spruce trees dotted around too.
The forest floor is often covered with anemones.
In May, when the beech trees burst into leaf,
people flock to the forests to collect beech twigs.
They put them in vases on their tables and mantlepieces.
They do that because the beech leaves tell them
that summer is not far away.

Many trees fall down in the autumn storms.
We have to clear the ground so that we can plant new trees.

My name is Poul
I'm an artist.

I live near the northern tip of Jutland at Skagen.
The landscape around here is beautiful.
The light is bright and the colours are very clear.
Many artists live and work in Skagen.
I built my own house and this is my studio.

Here is another room in my house.
I like to hang my paintings on the walls.

You are never far from the sea in Skagen.
All kinds of things get washed ashore on the beaches and
I often put these together to make interesting shapes.
Sometimes I make sculptures from driftwood.
In the winter we get strong west winds and then
the landscape looks very rough and bleak.
Not long ago houses used to be buried under sand
which was blown off the nearby sand dunes by the wind.
To make houses safer, trees were planted as windbreaks
and grass was grown to hold the sand in place.
There used to be bogs around here too, but
now they have been drained to make new farmland.

I'm Tina and I'm a sixth-former.

I am 18 years old and this is my last year at school.
I am studying science and this is the classroom
where we have our biology lessons.

Danish children start school when they are seven years old.

I live in a village just outside Ålborg in northern Jutland.
I catch the school bus at 7.30 every morning and
do my homework when I get back at 3.30 p.m.
I have to spend about three hours a day on homework
because I shall be taking my exams soon.
I shall be leaving school this summer and
I would like to train to be a nurse.
I may have to work in a nursing home for a year and then
try to get into a nursing college.
I don't work all the time of course.
I go to parties and I enjoy horse-riding.

I am Jørgen.
I'm a Mayor.

I have been the Mayor of Køge for the last eight years.
Køge is a busy port in Zealand.
I lead the town council and at the moment we are
working on plans to build new houses in the town.

Here I am
at my office desk
in the town hall.

Queen Margrethe II is the head of our Parliament.
Every other Monday the Queen will see anybody
who would like to talk to her.
Danish laws are made in our Parliament.
It is called the Folketing and it has 179 members.
There are 21 members of our town council in Køge.
We get grants from the government to help run Køge and
our main job is to spend this money wisely.

This is the Folketing where members meet
to discuss and pass new laws.

My name is Arne. I'm a soldier.

I'm a soldier in the Royal Life Guards in Copenhagen.
Our main duty is to protect the Queen and
other members of the Danish Royal Family.
We stand outside the Amalienborg and Fredensborg Palaces and
our orders are not to let in anyone we don't know.
Our rifles are always loaded with live bullets and
if a person doesn't stop we fire a warning shot into the air.
If they still don't stop we can shoot at them.
Luckily I've never had to do that.
We wear bearskins when we are on duty and
they can get pretty hot in summer.
My bearskin is about fifty years old.

This is the Amalienborg Palace in Copenhagen and
you can see the Life Guards on parade.

When I was a new soldier I had to train for three months.
I had to march up and down so many times that
I was worried that I wouldn't be able to keep going.

I'm Leo and I make clothes.

I have a clothing factory at Ikast in Jutland and there are 30 people working for me.
We make blouses, dresses and skirts in cotton or polyester.
Our blouses are very popular and many of our clothes are sold in other countries.

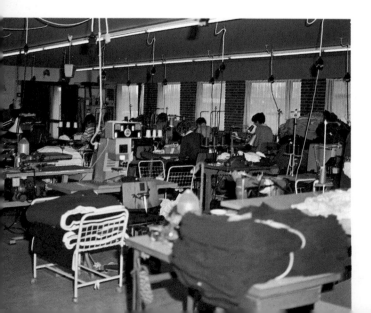

This is the sewing room at my factory.
It's hard to find people who are skilled at using a sewing machine.

Once or twice a year I go to Paris with my wife
to look at new clothes.
Paris is still the place to go if you want to find out
what's new in the fashion world.
We are always looking out for new designs.
When we make something new, the girls in the sewing room
test it for us.
I give them a T-shirt or a dress and
ask them to wear it for a while.
Then they tell me what the clothes are like.
If they are not happy with the clothes
we can alter them and make them better.

Some of our clothes are on sale at this shop.

My name is Bente and I am a tourist guide.

I trained to be a tourist guide in Copenhagen because
I thought it would help me to learn everyday English.
English is our second language in Denmark.
When I got a job as a guide
I enjoyed it so much that I stayed on.

◀ Our tourist information centre is in a large store in Copenhagen.

Vistors often want to know where they can hire a bike.
There are millions of bikes in Denmark because
the land is so flat.
There are cycle parks everywhere and some buses
even have a rack on the back to carry bikes.
Tourists come to Copenhagen all the year round.
In the winter they come to visit the theatre or the opera.
Copenhagen is also one of the best places in Europe to hear jazz.

Tourists and Danish people have great fun
at the Tivoli Park in Copenhagen.

I am Frede and I am a dairy worker.

I make butter in a dairy at Hjørring in Jutland.
Farmers send their cream to our dairy and
I control a churn that turns it into butter.

Tankers bring fresh cream to the dairy every day.

There are over a million cows in Denmark and
many of them are in Jutland.
Black-and-White Danish cows give the most milk but
we also get good milk from Jersey and Red Danish cows.
Every day 70 tonnes of cream arrive at the dairy and
from it we make 32 tonnes of butter.
First the cream is weighed.
Then it is heated and cooled to kill germs and
pumped into tanks where half the cream is turned sour.
The right amount of sour and 'sweet' cream
is then churned to make butter.

My name is John.
I'm a fitter.

I work at a shipyard at Elsinore in northern Zealand.
We make parts for ships' diesel engines.
I help to make new ships and repair damaged ones.
At the moment we are building four luxury liners which
will be sold to Iraq.

A lorry-load of steel parts
has just been delivered
to the Elsinore shipyard
where I work.

I am also a shop steward for the millers and turners
in the Metal Workers' Union.
Millers and turners use the machines which shape the metal
to make parts for ships' engines.
As shop steward I have to talk to the managers
about wages and problems the men have at work.
We've recently been having talks and
we shall soon get a small pay rise.

This is the workshop where ships' engine parts are made.

My name is Niels and I'm a market gardener.

My father started our market gardening business
at Lumby on Funen but now
my two brothers help me to run it.
The nursery has doubled in size since we took over.
Funen island is often called the 'Garden of Denmark' because
there are so many market gardens like ours.
We grow and sell a lot of ferns in pots.
We get the young plants from Holland and while they are growing
we have to make sure that they have enough water and that
the greenhouse is not too hot or too cold.
We also buy small banana plants from Israel.
It takes us six months to get them big enough for potting.
We sell potted plants to many European countries.

We also grow tulips
in our nursery.
As you can see,
they are grown outdoors.

This is one of our
large greenhouses.
We had blinds fitted
to the roof.
We draw them at night
to keep in the heat
and save fuel.

I'm Nukakuluk and I'm a social worker.

My job is to help people from Greenland
who are in hospital in Copenhagen.
Greenland is 3,000 km (2,000 miles) from here but
it is part of Denmark.
It is the largest island in the world.
I was born in Greenland but now I work in Denmark.

In Greenland the fishermen
have to watch out for
icebergs which can crush
their tiny boats.

Greenland is near the North Pole and it is covered
with ice and snow all the year round.

I hope to move back to Greenland one day soon.
My country is not at all like Denmark.
I miss the huge, peaceful open spaces.
Greenland is well-known for her cod, salmon, lamb,
furs, lead and zinc.
Greenland also has large amounts of iron ore and uranium and
if these were mined she would be a very rich country.

My name is Knud and I'm a ferryman.

I live in Assens which is a little town on Funen island.
There are 406 islands in Denmark.
In winter it can be a problem getting out
to the islands and back to the mainland.
The islands are often cut off because of the ice
that builds up between them.
I sail the ferry from Assens to the island of Baagø.
Every day I take seven children from Baagø
to their school on the mainland.
In spring I take seeds and fertilizers to the island's farmers.
In autumn I take the sugar beet the farmers have grown
to a sugar factory in Assens.

Here I am at the controls of the Assens to Baagø ferry. I have been a ferryman for 20 years.

We have just docked at Baagø and the cars are driving on board for the return trip. Baagø is a tiny island. Only 63 people live there.

My name is Kjeld.
I'm a baker.

I work at a bakery in Farum in Copenhagen.
I have two large ovens that can each bake 700 loaves.

I also make Danish pastries and here you can see me
putting the icing on top of them.

The bakery is behind this bread shop.
All my bread and cakes are freshly baked.

I bake many different kinds of wholemeal bread.
I make walnut bread and bread with sunflower seeds.
I also bake '4-in-1' bread which is made from four kinds of corn.
I make delicious cream-filled pastries too.
Not so many people buy them now because
they worry that the cream is too fattening and
bad for their health.

My name is Poul. and I'm an engine driver.

I have been working on the railways for over 30 years.
I started as a fireman on a steam train and one of my jobs
was to grease all the valves and connecting rods.

This is a modern
high-speed train
called the MZ.
We are using it on
the express route from
Copenhagen to Arhus.

Here I am in the cab of one of our new trains.

Modern trains are very different from the old steam trains.
Today I sit back in a comfortable seat and
the train skims quietly along the tracks.
I have a radio so that I can call for help in an emergency.
A few years ago a train got stuck in a snowdrift.
There was snow up to the windows and even inside the cab.
The driver had to be rescued by helicopter.

I am Jette.
I'm a weaver.

I weave carpets, tapestries and wall-hangings
in my workshop at Hasmark on Funen island.
My husband is a blacksmith and he has built
an electric spinning wheel on which I spin
the yarn for my tapestries.
At the moment I am working on altar hangings
and kneelers for a church.
The people at the church want everything to be just right
so I am taking great care with every sketch and sample.

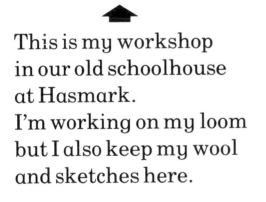

This is my workshop
in our old schoolhouse
at Hasmark.
I'm working on my loom
but I also keep my wool
and sketches here.

This is a wall-hanging
which I have just
finished for a customer.

I'm Inspector Larsen and I'm a policeman.

I work at Elsinore on the island of Zealand.
Elsinore is a port which is very close to Sweden
so all kinds of people pass through the town
and that means we are kept very busy.

Elsinore harbour
is one of the areas
I have to patrol.

There have been more robberies in recent years and
many of them have been violent.
More criminals now carry guns or long knives and
they don't seem to be afraid to use them.
Luckily we don't have to deal with violent criminals every day.
Most of our time is spent controlling marches,
settling small street fights, or coping with traffic jams.

We often have to control marches like this one.

I'm Kenneth and I'm a schoolboy.

I am 14 years old and I am in the fourth form
at a Danish comprehensive school.
I play in a football team and last year
we won the Zealand Championship.

Here in Denmark there is
plenty of snow in winter
for skiing but I'd rather
play football any day!

Even though I play a lot of football,
I don't want to become a professional.

Our team has been in the newspapers several times and
we were given a cup when we won the Championship.
I go training twice a week and we play a match once a week.
Denmark was the first country to start
a national football team in 1873.
Now there are 36 clubs in three divisions.
Badminton, cycling and swimming are all popular in Denmark.
It's important to learn to swim because Danish people
are never very far from the sea.

I am Finn and I'm an actor.

In 1972 some friends and I bought an old river barge and made it into a floating theatre.
We called it the Boat Theatre and it is moored at Nyhavn in Copenhagen.

This is the inside of the Boat Theatre. Today we are staging a children's play.

Copenhagen has 15 theatres and there are 10 in other cities.
There are also 40 travelling theatres.
The Royal Theatre in Copenhagen is the largest in Denmark.
About 60 shows a year are staged there.
You can see plays, ballet or opera at the Royal Theatre.
There are 45 actors, 90 dancers, 61 singers and
100 orchestra players working there.
Our Boat Theatre is not as large as that!

Here is the Boat Theatre at Nyhavn.

Facts

Capital City The capital city of Denmark
is Copenhagen.

Language Most people in Denmark speak Danish.
Greenlanders speak Eskimo.

Money Danish people pay for things with
ore and kroner.
There are 100 ore in 1 Danish kroner.

Churches Most Danish people belong to the
Danish Lutheran Church but
there are many other churches too.

People In 1980 there were over five million
people living in Denmark.
A quarter of them live in
and around Copenhagen.

Weather Denmark has very mild summers and
cold, wet winters.
The weather changes quickly because
Denmark is surrounded by sea.

Government Denmark has a Queen who is
Head of State.
Her name is Queen Margrethe II.
Denmark's Parliament is called
the Folketing.

Houses	Many people in Denmark own their own homes, which are often in high-rise buildings.
Schools	Most Danish children go to state schools called Folkeskolen or 'people's schools'. Some go to private schools and a few are taught at home.
Farming	Denmark sells butter, beef and bacon to other countries. Most of Denmark is farmland.
Factories	Factories in Denmark make packed foods, drinks, cement, ships, engines, chemicals, furniture, clothes, china and electrical goods.
News	All TV and radio broadcasting is run by *Danmarks Radio* which is state owned. There are no adverts on TV or radio. There are over 220 newspapers and 48 of them are daily papers.

Index